101 Words of Advice by Imam Abū Ḥanīfah

for Your Daily Life

Selected and Translated by:

ABDUL WAHAB SALEEM

ISBN978-0-9959261-1-0

Published by:

Salik Academy
www.SalikAcademy.com
books@salikacademy.com

بِسْمِ ٱللَّهِ ٱلرَّحْمَٰنِ ٱلرَّحِيمِ

In the name of Allah,
the One Who is Merciful [to all],
the One Who is Especially Merciful [to the believers].

Contents

PREFACE

~ Preface ~

All praise is due to Allah, the Lord of mankind and jinns.

The Messenger of Allah ﷺ had explicitly highlighted the virtue of the first three generations of Islam over those who will come after them by saying, "The people of my generation are the best, then those who follow them, and then who follow the latter."[1] [Al-Bukhārī & Muslim] It is in this spirit that I decided to select some of the wise words of Imam Abū Ḥanīfah رحمه الله who was among these early generations whom the Prophet ﷺ himself praised.

From the qualities for which Imam Abū Ḥanīfah رحمه الله was distinctly known was his wisdom. Some of the wisdom of the Imam that was accurately documented is found in two extensive counsels that he gave to two of his students, namely Abū Yūsuf al-Qāḍī رحمه الله and Yūsuf Ibn Khālid al-Samtī رحمه الله. However, advice to specific people by its very nature isn't always applicable to everyone. This is especially true in cases where the advised person has a very distinct role in society.

When studying the advice of Imam Abū Ḥanīfah رحمه الله to his two pupils, I noticed that some of the advice is general and is applicable to the lives of most people, whilst other pieces of advice appear particular to the context of his students, that time, and that culture.

For this reason, I decided to select and translate all of the pieces of advice given by the Imam to his two students which I believe are applicable to the lives of most people in our times in most contexts and situations. After the

1 *Sahih Muslim* 2533, and *Sahih al-Bukhari* 3651.

selection process, the accumulated number summed up to 101. It was a pleasant coincidence that the sum of the pieces of advice formed a number that also means "introductory" as the intent of this work is to present an introductory but deep and practical selection of advice for a Muslim's daily life.

I have also provided a brief biography of Abū Ḥanīfah رحمه الله to introduce this eminent Imam to the esteemed reader. I pray that you feel moved by the magnificence of this man and the brilliance of his wisdom, just as millions of his followers today around the world do.

May Allah bless you, enlighten your heart with wisdom, and grant you nobility. Amin!

Abdul Wahab Saleem
Shah Alam, Malaysia
10/30/2018

BIOGRAPHY OF IMĀM ABŪ ḤANĪFAH

رَحِمَهُ ٱللَّٰهُ

80 AH - 150 AH
699 CE - 767 CE

Biography of Imām Abū Ḥanīfah

Abū Ḥanīfah al-Nu'mān Ibn Thābit al-Taymī al-Kūfī رحمه الله was born in the year 80 AH / 699 CE during the era of the younger companions of the Messenger of Allah ﷺ. Among the companions who the Imam was blessed to meet was Anas Ibn Mālik رضي الله عنه. This means that Imam Abū Ḥanīfah رحمه الله was from the tābi'īn (the followers of the companions).[2] According to some scholars, the Imam also reported traditions from some of the companions[3]

We know that the generation of the *tābi'īn* has been highly regarded by the Messenger ﷺ. In addition to the Prophetic praise, Allah Himself praised this generation in the Quran by saying, ﴿As for the first emigrants (*muhājirīn*) and supporters (*anṣār*), **and those who followed them in goodness,** Allah is pleased with them and they are pleased with Allah. He has prepared for them gardens beneath which rivers flow, wherein they will live forever. That is the ultimate triumph.﴾ [9:100]

Surely it is great minds that pollinate and give birth to other great minds. Abu Hanifah رحمه الله had a fair share of great minds to learn from and be mentored by. Some sources mention that the list of his teachers extends to approximately 4000 teachers.[4]

Among these great mind was 'Aṭā' Ibn Abī Rabāḥ,

2 Most of the scholars of *ḥadīth* believe that simply meeting a companion is sufficient to be considered a *tābi'ī*. According to this group, extensive companionship, hearing reports from the companion, and being above the age of discerning are not conditions for one to be considered a *tābi'ī*. This is the opinion that Ibn Ḥajar al-'Asqalānī (r) prefered in *Nuzhat al-Naḍhar*. Based on this, Abū Ḥanīfah (ra) is definitely from the generation of the *tābi'īn*.

3 *I'lā' al-Sunan*, 21-22/6-11.

4 *Sharḥ Musnad Abī Ḥanīfah*, Al-Mullā 'Alī al-Qārī, 8.

Rabāḥ (r), al-Sha'bī, Nāfi', Qatādah, Ḥammād Ibn Abī Sulaymān, Hishām Ibn 'Urwah, Ibn Shihāb al-Zuhrī and many others. In fact, Imam Abū Ḥanīfah was so keen on seeking knowledge that he even learned from scholars who were younger than him. Among the younger scholars from whom Abū Ḥanīfah reported is Imam Mālik himself. May Allah have His mercy on all of them.

Just as he had many teachers, he also had many students. The learners of his era raced to learn from the Imam because of his distinct ability to dissect information. Al-Dhahabī ﵀ writes commenting on this distinct ability, "In terms of *fiqh*, and scrutinizing opinions, and subtleties, he is the limit. People are all in need of him in this regard."[5] It was precisely because of this ability that Imam al-Dhahabī ﵀ himself granted Abū Ḥanīfah ﵀ the title,

"فقيه الملة / The Jurist of the Nation."[6]

This title was only granted by al-Dhahabī ﵀ to two people throughout his encyclopedia which comprises biographies of nearly 6000 figures in Islamic history. One of the two was Imam Abū Ḥanīfah ﵀.

Of the most prized graduates from the school of this great Imam were Abū Yūsuf al-Qāḍī ﵀, and Muḥammad Ibn al-Ḥasan al-Shaybānī ﵀. These two students, who are great scholars in their own right, became the torchbearers of Abū Ḥanīfah's legal school of thought.

To the scholars of the Ḥanafī school of thought, they are known as *al-Ṣāḥibān*, the two companions of Imam

5 *Siyar A'lām al-Nubalā'*, al-Dhahabī, 6/392.

6 Ibid., 6/390.

Abū Ḥanīfah ﷺ. They also refer to the trio as "Our Three Imams". Moreover, they may refer to one of the three Imams, as *al-Awwal* (the first), *al-Thānī* (the second), and *al-Thālith* (the third). *Al-Awwal* being Imam Abū Ḥanīfah ﷺ, *al-Thānī* being Abū Yūsuf al-Qāḍī ﷺ, and *al-Thālith* being Muḥammad Ibn al-Ḥasan al-Shaybānī ﷺ. Such particular titles for these two students of Imam Abū Ḥanīfah ﷺ specifically shows their significance and prominence.[7]

Additionally, many of the finest traditionists (*muḥaddithīn*) in history were from the pupils of Abū Ḥanīfah ﷺ and they greatly appreciated their tutelage under the Imam. One such traditionist by the name of 'Abdullāh Ibn al-Mubārak ﷺ expressed his immense gratitude for having studied with Imam Abū Ḥanīfah ﷺ by saying, "If it wasn't for the fact that Allah helped me through Abū Ḥanīfah and Sufyān, I would be like the rest of the people."[8]

Furthermore, his noble status was well known to the founders of the four schools of thought. For example, Imam al-Shāfi'ī ﷺ asked Imam Mālik ﷺ, "Did you see Abū Ḥanīfah?" Imam Malik ﷺ replied, "I saw a man [who was so intelligent] that were he to attempt to convince you that this pillar is made of gold, he would be able to do so."[9]

In addition to being a man of great knowledge, he was a man of great piety. The immense scrupulousness (*wara'*) of Imam Abū Ḥanīfah ﷺ was such that he would refuse to sit in the shade of a wall of his debtor out of fear that the debtor only allowed him to take shade under his wall because of the debt which may be understood as usury.

---

7 *Al-Madkhal 'Ilā al-Madh-hab al-Ḥanafī*, Muḥammad Rashād Manṣūr Shams, 51-52.

8 Ibid., 6/398.

9 Ibid., 6/399.

Explaining this action, he would say: "He owes me some money and any debt which leads to a benefit is usury. Me sitting in the shade of his wall is me benefiting from his wall."[10]

Moreover, Imam Abū Ḥanīfah ﵀ was a man of great worship and servitude. Asad Ibn 'Amr reported that Abū Ḥanīfah ﵀ prayed 'Ishā' and Fajr with the same ablution for forty consecutive years. This means that he would be up all night busy with the worship of Allah from 'Ishā' to Fajr which enabled him to employ the ablution of 'Ishā' to pray Fajr as well.[11] For this reason, some used to refer to him as a 'post' because of how long he would stay stationary in one place praying to Allah.

He is described as a person of average height, handsome, eloquent, melodious, clear, slightly brown, and regularly perfumed. He was a composed man who wouldn't speak except when spoken to. He wouldn't involve himself in things that didn't concern him. He was also known to be very generous. Whenever he would spend money on his family, he would ensure to spend the same amount in charity.[12]

People of such great virtue are rarely left untested by Allah as the patience that one has during trials and tribulations further raises a person's status. The Messenger of Allah ﷺ was once asked, "O Messenger of Allah ﷺ, which of the people are tested most?" He replied, "The Prophets, then the best after them, then the best after them. A man is tried according to [the strength of] his faith. If his faith is firm, his trials become more severe, and if his faith is weak, his trials are accordingly. The slave [of Allah] shall

10 *Al-Mīzān al-Kubrā*, al-Sha'rānī, 1/87.

11 *Siyar A'lām al-Nubalā'*, al-Dhahabī, 6/399.

12 Ibid., 6/400.

constantly be tried until he is left walking upon the earth without any sins.”[13]

One of the trials of Abū Ḥanīfah ﷺ occured when he was asked by prince Ibn Hubairah to become a judge. However, Abū Ḥanīfah ﷺ insisted on evading such a position considering the significance of the role and the difficulty in fulfilling such a trust (*amānah*). In response to the refusal of Abū Ḥanīfah ﷺ, the prince commanded for him to be lashed. The esteemed Imam was lashed for several days. Historical records tell us that the Imam ﷺ was struck with a total of 110 lashes. However, he adamantly continued to refuse the position.[14]

Even within such trials, the distinct intellect of the Imam became evident. Abū Ja'far al-Manṣūr, the caliph of that time, summoned the Imam from Kufa to Baghdad to discuss his refusal to become a judge. Abū Ja'far said, “Do you wish to oppose our system?” The Imam replied, “May Allah rectify the leader of the believers. I am not appropriate to become a judge. ” Abū Ja'far responded, “You're lying!” The caliph then reiterated the offer. To this, the Imam replied, “The leader of the believers has rendered me incapable of being a judge. He called me a liar. If I am a liar, I am not appropriate to serve as a judge, and if I am truthful, I've already informed the leader of the believers that I'm not appropriate [for the job].” The Imam was then returned to prison.[15]

When one reads this trial of Abū Ḥanīfah ﷺ today, it almost doesn't make sense that for such a simple reason, a scholar of his caliber and esteem would end up in jail

13 *Jāmi' al-Tirmidhī* 2398.

14 *Tārīkh Baghdād*, al-Khaṭīb al-Baghdādī, 15/444.

15 Ibid., 15/444.

and be humiliated in such ways. However, those who had humiliated him are forgotten today, whereas Imam Abū Ḥanīfah ﷺ is perhaps the most famous Imam known to the *ummah* around the world. Likewise, those who humiliate, oppress, torture, and even murder the sincere scholars of Islam today using their authority in oppressive ways will be forgotten. However, the legacy of the sincere heirs of the Messenger ﷺ will live on as it is but an extension to the legacy of the Messenger ﷺ himself.

There is much more to say about the life of this great Imam. However, I do not wish for an extensive biography to complicate the intended simplicity of this work, nor do I wish to delay the reader any longer from directly experiencing the intellect of this man about whom ʿAlī Ibn ʿĀṣim said, ❝If the intellect of Abū Ḥanīfah ﷺ was to be weighed against the intellect of half of the people of the world, it would outweigh it.❞[16] In short, the virtues of this great man can be summed up by the words of Yazīd Ibn Hārūn ﷺ who said, ❝I met [many] people, but I never saw anyone more intelligent, virtuous, and scropolous than Abū Ḥanīfah.❞[17]

His long life of worship, learning, teaching, and generosity came to its inevitable end in the year 150 AH, the same year in which Imam Al-Shāfiʿī ﷺ was born. I'm well aware that some people in the past and the present have attempted to diminish the great status of Imam Abū Ḥanīfah ﷺ. Perhaps, this is a test that Allah has placed the Imam in to further raise his status even after his death.

By divine decree, Allah had made within his death itself many signs of his great virtue. For example, Allah

16 Ibid., 15/487.

17 Ibid., 15/487.

had granted the Imam the status of martyrdom because he was poisoned to death. Imam al-Dhahabī said, "He died a martyr as he was poisoned."[18]

Among many other factors that emphasize his virtuous death, the burial of Abū Ḥanīfah ﵀ stands witness to the type of acceptance that Allah had placed in the hearts of the people for this eminent Imam. Imam Aḥmad ﵀ once said in regards to the innovators during his era, "Say to the people of innovation: the deciding moment between us and you will be the funerals!"[19] The funeral of Imam Abū Ḥanīfah ﵀ was attended by so many people that there wasn't enough room for everyone to pray all at once. It took six separate funeral prayers for all of the people who attended to be accommodated.

The public was so keen on attending this *janāzah* that his son wasn't able to pray upon his own father until the sixth funeral prayer. Furthermore, people continued to pray *janāzah* on his grave after his burial for twenty days.[20]

May Allah have His mercy on Imam Abū Ḥanīfah and all the great Imams and scholars of Islam. May they live in peace, die in peace, rest in peace, be resurrected in peace, and be admitted to the abode of peace. Amin!

18 *Siyar A'lām al-Nubalā'*, al-Dhahabī, 6/403.

19 Ibid., 11/340.

20 *Akhbār Abī Ḥanīfah*, al-Ṣaymarī, 93.

Selections from the Advice *of* Imam Abū Ḥanifah *to* Yūsuf Ibn Khālid Al-Samtī

Abū Ḥanīfah رحمه الله said:

"Wear new clothes and regularly wear perfume."

Personal Reflections

قال أبو حنيفة رحمه الله:

«اسْتَجِدَّ ثِيَابَكَ وَأَكْثِرِ اسْتِعْمَالَ الطِّيبِ.»

ABŪ ḤANĪFAH رَحِمَهُ ٱللَّٰهُ SAID:

"Make some private time for yourself in which you sort your own needs out."

PERSONAL REFLECTIONS

____

____

____

____

____

____

قال أبو حنيفة رَحِمَهُ ٱللَّٰهُ:

«وَاجْعَلْ لِنَفْسِكَ خَلْوَةً تَرُمُّ بِهَا حَوَائِجَكَ.»

Abū Ḥanīfah رَحِمَهُ ٱللَّٰهُ said:

“Observe your prayers.”

Personal Reflections

قال أبو حنيفة رَحِمَهُ ٱللَّٰهُ:

«وَحَافِظْ عَلَى صَلَوَاتِكَ.»

ABŪ ḤANĪFAH رحمه الله SAID:

"Be generous with your food as a miser never prevails."

PERSONAL REFLECTIONS

قال أبو حنيفة رحمه الله:

«وَابْذُلْ طَعَامَكَ فَإِنَّهُ مَا سَادَ بَخِيلٌ قَطُّ.»

Abū Ḥanīfah رَحِمَهُ ٱللَّهُ said:

“Be forgiving, and command good!”

Personal Reflections

قال أبو حنيفة رَحِمَهُ ٱللَّهُ:

«وَخُذِ العَفْوَ وَأْمُرْ بِالمَعْرُوفِ.»

ABŪ ḤANĪFAH رَحِمَهُ اللهُ SAID:

“Ignore whatever is of no concern to you.”

PERSONAL REFLECTIONS

قال أبو حنيفة رَحِمَهُ اللهُ:

«تَغَافَلْ عَمَّا لَا يَعْنِيكَ.»

Abū Ḥanīfah رَحِمَهُ ٱللَّٰهُ said:

"Leave everyone who harms you."

Personal Reflections

قال أبو حنيفة رَحِمَهُ ٱللَّٰهُ:

«وَاتْرُكْ كُلَّ مَنْ يُؤْذِيكَ.»

ABŪ ḤANĪFAH رحمه الله SAID:

"Honour the people of nobility."

PERSONAL REFLECTIONS

قال أبو حنيفة رحمه الله:

«وَأَكْرِمْ أَهْلَ الشَّرَفِ.»

Abū Ḥanīfah رحمه الله said:

"Honour the people of knowledge."

Personal Reflections

قال أبو حنيفة رحمه الله:

«وَعَظِّمْ أَهْلَ العِلْمِ.»

ABŪ ḤANĪFAH رَحِمَهُ ٱللَّهُ SAID:

"Respect the elderly."

PERSONAL REFLECTIONS

قال أبو حنيفة رَحِمَهُ ٱللَّهُ:

«وَوَقِّرِ الشُّيُوخَ.»

Abū Ḥanīfah رَحِمَهُ ٱللَّٰهُ said:

“Be kind to youngsters.”

Personal Reflections

قال أبو حنيفة رَحِمَهُ ٱللَّٰهُ:

«وَلَاطِفِ الأَحْدَاثَ.»

ABŪ ḤANĪFAH رَحِمَهُ ٱللَّهُ SAID:

"Deflect the immoral through appeasement."

PERSONAL REFLECTIONS

____

____

____

____

____

____

قال أبو حنيفة رَحِمَهُ ٱللَّهُ:

«وَدَارِ الفُجَّارَ.»

Abū Ḥanīfah رَحِمَهُ ٱللَّٰهُ said:

“Accompany the best.”

Personal Reflections

قال أبو حنيفة رَحِمَهُ ٱللَّٰهُ:

«وَاصْحَبِ الأَخْيَارَ.»

Abū Ḥanīfah رحمه الله said:

“Don’t degrade the sultan.”

Personal Reflections

قال أبو حنيفة رحمه الله:

«وَلَا تتَهَاوَنْ بِالسُّلْطَانِ.»

Abū Ḥanīfah رحمه الله said:

“Don’t belittle anyone who approaches you.”

Personal Reflections

قال أبو حنيفة رحمه الله:

«وَلَا تَحْقِرَنَّ أَحَدًا يَقْصِدُكَ.»

ABŪ ḤANĪFAH رَحِمَهُ ٱللَّهُ SAID:

"Don't be negligent in showing your love [to those who approach you]."

PERSONAL REFLECTIONS

____

____

____

____

____

____

قال أبو حنيفة رَحِمَهُ ٱللَّهُ:

«وَلَا تُقَصِّرَنَّ فِي إِقَامَةِ مَوَدَّتِكَ إِيَّاهُمْ.»

Abū Ḥanīfah رَحِمَهُ ٱللَّٰهُ said:

“Don’t share your secrets with anyone.”

Personal Reflections

قال أبو حنيفة رَحِمَهُ ٱللَّٰهُ:

«وَلَا تُخْرِجَنَّ سِرَّكَ إِلَى أَحَدٍ.»

ABŪ ḤANĪFAH رَحِمَهُ ٱللَّهُ SAID:

"Don't trust anyone's companionship until you test them."

PERSONAL REFLECTIONS

قال أبو حنيفة رَحِمَهُ ٱللَّهُ:

«وَلَا تَثِقَنَّ بِصُحْبَةِ أَحَدٍ حَتَّى تَمْتَحِنَهُ.»

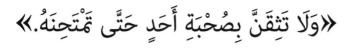

Abū Ḥanīfah رحمه الله said:

"Don't hire an ignoble or vile servant."

Personal Reflections

قال أبو حنيفة رحمه الله:

«وَلَا تُخَادِمْ خَسِيسًا وَلَا وَضِيعًا.»

ABŪ ḤANĪFAH رَحِمَهُ ٱللَّٰهُ SAID:

"Don't say something which appears rejectable."

PERSONAL REFLECTIONS

قال أبو حنيفة رَحِمَهُ ٱللَّٰهُ :

«وَلَا تَقُولَنَّ مِنَ الكَلَامِ مَا يُنْكَرُ عَلَيكَ فِي ظَاهِرِهِ.»

Abū Ḥanīfah رحمه الله said:

"Don't open up to foolish people."

Personal Reflections

قال أبو حنيفة رحمه الله:

«وَإِيَّاكَ وَالانْبِسَاطَ إِلَى السُّفَهَاءِ.»

ABŪ ḤANĪFAH رَحِمَهُ ٱللَّهُ SAID:

"Appease and adopt patience, forbearance, good character, and lenience."

PERSONAL REFLECTIONS

قال أبو حنيفة رَحِمَهُ ٱللَّهُ:

«وَعَليكَ بِالمُدَارَاةِ، وَالصَّبْرِ، وَالاحْتِمَالِ، وَحُسْنِ الخُلُقِ، وَسَعَةِ الصَّدْرِ.»

Abū Ḥanīfah رحمه الله said:

"Seek out the news of your servants and proceed to correct and discipline them."

Personal Reflections

قال أبو حنيفة رحمه الله:

«وَابْحَثْ عَنْ أَخْبَارِ حَشَمِكَ، وَتَقَدَّمْ فِي تَقْوِيمِهِمْ وَتَأْدِيبِهِمْ.»

Abū Ḥanīfah رَحِمَهُ ٱللَّهُ said:

“[However], be kind when you [do correct them].”

Personal Reflections

____

____

____

____

____

____

قال أبو حنيفة رَحِمَهُ ٱللَّهُ:

«وَاسْتَعْمِلْ فِي ذَلِكَ الرِّفْقَ.»

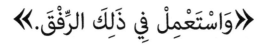

Abū Ḥanīfah رحمه الله said:

"Don't admonish too much lest censure lose its value."

Personal Reflections

قال أبو حنيفة رحمه الله:

«وَلَا تُكْثِرِ العَتْبَ فَيَهُونَ العَذْلُ.»

ABŪ ḤANĪFAH رحمه الله SAID:

"Don't discipline [your servants] yourself as that will maintain your respect and awe."

PERSONAL REFLECTIONS

قال أبو حنيفة رحمه الله:

«وَلَا تَلِ تَأْدِيبَهُمْ بِنَفْسِكَ، فَإِنَّهُ أَبْقَى لِمَائِكَ، وَأَهْيَبُ لَكَ.»

Abū Ḥanīfah رَحِمَهُ ٱللَّهُ said:

"Visit those who visit you and those who don't. Be kind to those who are kind to you and those who wrong you."

Personal Reflections

قال أبو حنيفة رَحِمَهُ ٱللَّهُ:

«وَاعْمِدْ فِي زِيَارَةِ مَنْ يَزُورُكَ وَمَنْ لَا يَزُورُكَ،

وَالإِحْسَانِ إِلَى مَنْ أَحْسَنَ إِلَيكَ وَمَنْ أَسَاءَ.»

ABŪ ḤANĪFAH رحمه الله SAID:

"Hasten to fulfil the rights [of others]."

PERSONAL REFLECTIONS

قال أبو حنيفة رحمه الله:

«وَبَادِرْ فِي إِقَامَةِ الحُقُوقِ.»

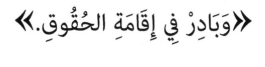

Abū Ḥanīfah رَحِمَهُ ٱللَّهُ said:

"Whoever falls ill from your brothers, visit him yourself and provide him care through your representatives."

Personal Reflections

قال أبو حنيفة رَحِمَهُ ٱللَّهُ:

«وَمَنْ مَرِضَ مِنْ إِخْوَانِكَ فَعُدْهُ بِنَفْسِكَ، وَتَعَاهَدْهُ بِرُسُلِكَ.»

ABŪ ḤANĪFAH رَحِمَهُ ٱللَّٰهُ SAID:

"Connect with those who have forsaken you."

PERSONAL REFLECTIONS

قال أبو حنيفة رَحِمَهُ ٱللَّٰهُ:

«وَصِلْ مَنْ جَفَاكَ.»

Abū Ḥanīfah رَحِمَهُ ٱللَّٰهُ said:

"Honour those who come to you."

Personal Reflections

قال أبو حنيفة رَحِمَهُ ٱللَّٰهُ:

«وَأَكْرِمْ مَنْ أَتَاكَ.»

ABŪ ḤANĪFAH رَحِمَهُ ٱللَّهُ SAID:

"Pardon those who have wronged you."

PERSONAL REFLECTIONS

قال أبو حنيفة رَحِمَهُ ٱللَّهُ:

«وَاعْفُ عَمَّنْ أَسَاءَ إِلَيكَ.»

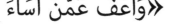

Abū Ḥanīfah رحمه الله said:

“Whoever speaks ill of you, say beautiful things about them.”

Personal Reflections

قال أبو حنيفة رحمه الله:

«وَمَنْ تَكَلَّمَ مِنْهُمْ بِالقَبِيحِ فِيكَ، فَتَكَلَّمْ فِيهِ بِالحَسَنِ الجَمِيلِ.»

ABŪ ḤANĪFAH رَحِمَهُ ٱللَّٰهُ SAID:

"Fulfill the rights of the one who has died."

PERSONAL REFLECTIONS

قال أبو حنيفة رَحِمَهُ ٱللَّٰهُ:

«وَمَنْ مَاتَ قَضَيتَ لَهُ حَقَّهُ.»

Abū Ḥanīfah رَحِمَهُ ٱللَّهُ said:

"If someone has a joyful occasion, congratulate them."

Personal Reflections

قال أبو حنيفة رَحِمَهُ ٱللَّهُ:

«وَمَنْ كَانَتْ لَهُ فَرْحَةٌ، هَنِّيتَهُ بِهَا.»

ABŪ ḤANĪFAH رَحِمَهُ ٱللَّٰهُ SAID:

"If someone has a difficulty, console him."

PERSONAL REFLECTIONS

قال أبو حنيفة رَحِمَهُ ٱللَّٰهُ:

«وَمَنْ كَانَتْ لَهُ مُصِيبَةٌ، عَزِّيَتَهُ بِهَا.»

Abū Ḥanīfah رحمه الله said:

“If someone is aggrieved, then show them sympathy.”

Personal Reflections

قال أبو حنيفة رحمه الله:

«وَمَنْ أَصَابَهُ هَمٌّ، فَتَوَجَّعْ لَهُ بِهَا.»

ABŪ ḤANĪFAH رَحِمَهُ ٱللَّهُ SAID:

"If someone urges you to stand for some of his needs, stand with him!"

PERSONAL REFLECTIONS

قال أبو حنيفة رَحِمَهُ ٱللَّهُ:

«وَمَنِ اسْتَنْهَضَكَ لِأَمْرٍ مِنْ أُمُورِهِ، نَهَضْتَ لَهُ.»

Abū Ḥanīfah رَحِمَهُ ٱللَّٰهُ said:

"If someone asks for your aid, aid him!"

Personal Reflections

قال أبو حنيفة رَحِمَهُ ٱللَّٰهُ:

«وَمَنِ اسْتَغَاثَكَ فَأَغِثْهُ.»

ABŪ ḤANĪFAH رَحِمَهُ ٱللَّهُ SAID:

"If someone seeks your help, help him!"

PERSONAL REFLECTIONS

قال أبو حنيفة رَحِمَهُ ٱللَّهُ:

«وَمَنِ اسْتَنْصَرَكَ، فَانْصُرْهُ.»

Abū Ḥanīfah رحمه الله said:

"Show love to the people as much as you can."

Personal Reflections

____

____

____

____

____

____

قال أبو حنيفة رحمه الله:

«وَأَظْهِرِ التَّوَدُّدَ إِلَى النَّاسِ مَا اسْتَطَعْتَ.»

Abū Ḥanīfah رحمه الله said:

"Spread *salām* even to those who happen to be wicked."

Personal Reflections

قال أبو حنيفة رحمه الله:

«وَأَفْشِ السَّلَامَ، وَلَوْ عَلَى قَوْمٍ لِئَامٍ.»

Abū Ḥanīfah رحمه الله said:

“Treat people the way you would treat yourself.”

Personal Reflections

____

____

____

____

____

____

قال أبو حنيفة رحمه الله:

«وَعَـامِلِ النَّاسَ مُعَامَلَتَكَ نَفْسَكَ.»

ABŪ ḤANĪFAH رحمه الله SAID:

"Help your soul by maintaining it and observing its state."

PERSONAL REFLECTIONS

قال أبو حنيفة رحمه الله:

«وَاسْتَعِنْ عَلَى نَفْسِكَ بِالصِّيَانَةِ لَهَا وَالمُرَاقَبَةِ لِأَحْوَالِهَا.»

Abū Ḥanīfah رَحِمَهُ ٱللَّٰهُ said:

"Don't show your annoyance to someone who doesn't show his annoyance to you."

Personal Reflections

____

____

____

____

____

____

قال أبو حنيفة رَحِمَهُ ٱللَّٰهُ:

«وَلَا تَضْجَرْ لِمَنْ لَا يَضْجَرُ عَلَيْكَ.»

ABŪ ḤANĪFAH رَحِمَهُ اللهُ SAID:

"Don't cause problems."

PERSONAL REFLECTIONS

قال أبو حنيفة رَحِمَهُ اللهُ:

«وَدَعِ الشَّغَبَ.»

Abū Ḥanīfah رحمه الله said:

"Listen to those who listen to you."

Personal Reflections

قال أبو حنيفة رحمه الله:

«وَاسْتَمِعْ لِمَنْ يَسْتَمِعُ مِنْكَ.»

Abū Ḥanīfah رَحِمَهُ ٱللَّٰهُ said:

“Don’t burden people what they don’t burden you with.”

Personal Reflections

قال أبو حنيفة رَحِمَهُ ٱللَّٰهُ:

«وَلَا تُكَلِّفِ النَّاسَ مَا لَا يُكَلِّفُوكَ.»

Abū Ḥanīfah رحمه الله said:

"Prioritize a good intention."

Personal Reflections

قال أبو حنيفة رحمه الله:

«وَقَدِّمْ حُسْنَ النِّيَّةِ.»

ABŪ ḤANĪFAH رَحِمَهُ ٱللَّٰهُ SAID:

"Do away with arrogance."

PERSONAL REFLECTIONS

قال أبو حنيفة رَحِمَهُ ٱللَّٰهُ:

«وَاطْرَحِ الكِبْرَ جَانِبًا.»

Abū Ḥanīfah رَحِمَهُ ٱللَّهُ said:

“Don’t betray even if someone betrays you.”

Personal Reflections

قال أبو حنيفة رَحِمَهُ ٱللَّهُ:

«وَإِيَّاكَ وَالغَدْرَ وَإِنْ غَدَرُوا بِكَ.»

ABŪ ḤANĪFAH رَحِمَهُ ٱللَّٰهُ SAID:

“Fulfil the trust even with those who have cheated you.”

PERSONAL REFLECTIONS

قال أبو حنيفة رَحِمَهُ ٱللَّٰهُ:

«وَأَدِّ الأَمَانَةَ وَإِنْ خَانُوكَ.»

Abū Ḥanīfah رَحِمَهُ ٱللَّهُ said:

"Cling to loyalty."

∞ · ***Personal Reflections*** · ∞

____

____

____

____

____

____

قال أبو حنيفة رَحِمَهُ ٱللَّهُ:

«وَتَمَسَّكْ بِالوَفَاءِ.»

ABŪ ḤANĪFAH رحمه الله SAID:

“Keep to piety.”

PERSONAL REFLECTIONS

قال أبو حنيفة رحمه الله:

«وَاعْتَصِمْ بِالتَّقْوَى.»

Abū Ḥanīfah رَحِمَهُ ٱللَّٰهُ said:

"Treat the people of other religions the way they treat you."

Personal Reflections

قال أبو حنيفة رَحِمَهُ ٱللَّٰهُ:

«وَعَاشِرْ أَهْلَ الأَدْيَانِ حَسَبَ مُعَاشَرَتِهِمْ لَكَ.»

Selections from the Advice *of* Imam Abū Ḥanifah *to* Abū Yūsuf Al-Qāḍī

Abū Ḥanīfah رحمه الله said:

"Respect the sultan, and honour his status."

Personal Reflections

قال أبو حنيفة رحمه الله:

«وَقِّرِ السُّلْطَانَ وَعَظِّمْ مَنْزِلَتَهُ.»

ABŪ ḤANĪFAH رَحِمَهُ ٱللَّهُ SAID:

“Don’t be ashamed to speak the truth, even if it be before a sultan.”

PERSONAL REFLECTIONS

قال أبو حنيفة رَحِمَهُ ٱللَّهُ:

«وَلَا تَحْتَشِمْ مِنْ أَحَدٍ عِنْدَ ذِكْرِ الحَقِّ؛ وَإِنْ كَانَ سُلْطَانًا.»

Abū Ḥanīfah رَحِمَهُ ٱللَّٰهُ said:

“Do not excessively go to the markets.”

Personal Reflections

قال أبو حنيفة رَحِمَهُ ٱللَّٰهُ:

«وَلَا تُكْثِرِ الخُرُوجَ إِلَى الأَسْوَاقِ.»

Abū Ḥanīfah رَحِمَهُ ٱللَّٰهُ said:

"Don't sit around in the middle of the streets, and if you must then sit in the mosque."

Personal Reflections

قال أبو حنيفة رَحِمَهُ ٱللَّٰهُ:

«وَلَا تَقْعُدْ عَلَى قَوَارِعِ الطَّرِيقِ، فَإِذَا دَعَاكَ ذَلِكَ فَاقْعُدْ فِي المَسْجِدِ.»

Abū Ḥanīfah رحمه الله said:

“Adopt consciousness (taqwā) of Allah, fulfil the trust, and adopt sincerity for all elite and general people.”

Personal Reflections

قال أبو حنيفة رحمه الله:

«وَعَلَيْكَ بِتَقْوَى اللَّهِ، وَأَدَاءِ الأَمَانَةِ،
وَالنَّصِيحَةِ لِجَمِيعِ الخَاصَّةِ وَالعَامَّةِ.»

Abū Ḥanīfah رَحِمَهُ ٱللَّهُ said:

"Do not belittle people. Honour yourself and honour them."

Personal Reflections

قال أبو حنيفة رَحِمَهُ ٱللَّهُ:

«وَلَا تَسْتَخِفَّ بِالنَّاسِ، وَوَقِّرْ نَفْسَكَ وَوَقِّرْهُمْ.»

Abū Ḥanīfah رَحِمَهُ ٱللَّٰهُ said:

“Be careful of the people!”

Personal Reflections

قال أبو حنيفة رَحِمَهُ ٱللَّٰهُ:

«وَكُنْ مِنَ النَّاسِ عَلَى حَذَرٍ!»

ABŪ ḤANĪFAH رَحِمَهُ ٱللَّٰهُ SAID:

"Be with Allah inwardly just as you are with Him outwardly."

PERSONAL REFLECTIONS

____

____

____

____

____

____

قال أبو حنيفة رَحِمَهُ ٱللَّٰهُ:

«وَكُنْ لِلّٰهِ فِي سِرِّكَ كَمَا أَنْتَ لَهُ فِي عَلَانِيَتِكَ.»

Abū Ḥanīfah رحمه الله said:

"Knowledge can never be maintained except if you make its inward state the same as you do outwardly."

Personal Reflections

قال أبو حنيفة رحمه الله:

«وَلَا يَصْلُحُ أَمْرُ العِلْمِ إِلَّا بَعْدَ أَنْ تَجْعَلَ سِرَّهُ كَعَلَانِيَتِهِ.»

ABŪ ḤANĪFAH رَحِمَهُ ٱللَّٰهُ SAID:

“Don’t laugh too much as that kills the heart.”

PERSONAL REFLECTIONS

قال أبو حنيفة رَحِمَهُ ٱللَّٰهُ:

«وَإِيَّاكَ أَنْ تُكْثِرَ الضَّحِكَ؛ فَإِنَّهُ يُمِيتُ القَلْبَ.»

Abū Ḥanīfah رَحِمَهُ ٱللَّٰهُ said:

“Don’t walk except with tranquility.”

Personal Reflections

قال أبو حنيفة رَحِمَهُ ٱللَّٰهُ:

«وَلَا تَمْشِ إِلَّا عَلَى طُمَأْنِينَةٍ.»

Abū Ḥanīfah رحمه الله said:

"Don't be hasty in [your] matters."

Personal Reflections

____

____

____

____

____

____

قال أبو حنيفة رحمه الله:

«وَلَا تَكُنْ عَجُولًا فِي الأُمُورِ.»

Abū Ḥanīfah رحمه الله said:

“When you speak, don’t scream too much, and don’t raise your voice.”

Personal Reflections

___

___

___

___

___

___

قال أبو حنيفة رحمه الله:

«وَإِذَا تَكَلَّمْتَ، فَلَا تُكْثِرْ صِيَاحَكَ، وَلَا تَرْفَعْ صَوتَكَ.»

ABŪ ḤANĪFAH رَحِمَهُ ٱللَّهُ SAID:

"Make tranquility and the lack of movement your habit so that people become ascertained of your stability."

PERSONAL REFLECTIONS

____

____

____

____

____

____

قال أبو حنيفة رَحِمَهُ ٱللَّهُ:

«وَاتَّخِذْ لِنَفْسِكَ السُّكُونَ وَقِلَّةَ الحَرَكَةِ عَادَةً، كَيْ يَتَحَقَّقَ عِنْدَ النَّاسِ ثَبَاتُكَ.»

Abū Ḥanīfah رحمه الله said:

“Don’t follow the mistakes of people, rather follow their sound views.”

Personal Reflections

قال أبو حنيفة رحمه الله:

«وَلَا تَتَّبِعِ النَّاسَ فِي خَطَئِهِمْ، بَلْ اتَّبِعْهُمْ فِي صَوَابِهِمْ.»

ABŪ ḤANĪFAH رَحِمَهُ ٱللَّهُ SAID:

"Don't sit with the people of desires (innovations) except to call them to the religion."

PERSONAL REFLECTIONS

____

____

____

____

____

____

قال أبو حنيفة رَحِمَهُ ٱللَّهُ:

«وَلَا تُجَالِسْ أَحَدًا مِنْ أَهْلِ الْأَهْوَاءِ إِلَّا عَلَى سَبِيلِ الدَّعْوَةِ إِلَى الدِّينِ.»

Abū Ḥanīfah رحمه الله said:

"Don't play or insult excessively."

Personal Reflections

قال أبو حنيفة رحمه الله:

«وَلَا تُكْثِرِ اللَّعِبَ وَالشَّتْمَ.»

ABŪ ḤANĪFAH رَحِمَهُ ٱللَّهُ SAID:

"If you notice [a mistake] of your neighbour, conceal it for him as it's a trust!"

PERSONAL REFLECTIONS

قال أبو حنيفة رَحِمَهُ ٱللَّهُ:

«وَمَا رَأَيْتَ عَلَى جَارِكَ فَاسْتُرْهُ عَلَيْهِ فَإِنَّهُ أَمَانَةٌ!»

Abū Ḥanīfah رحمه الله said:

“Don’t reveal the secrets of people.”

Personal Reflections

قال أبو حنيفة رحمه الله:

«وَلَا تُظْهِرْ أَسْرَارَ النَّاسِ.»

ABŪ ḤANĪFAH رَحِمَهُ ٱللَّهُ SAID:

"Whoever consults you in a matter, direct him to whatever you think will bring you closer to Allah."

PERSONAL REFLECTIONS

قال أبو حنيفة رَحِمَهُ ٱللَّهُ:

«وَمَنِ اسْتَشَارَكَ فِي شَيْءٍ، فَأَشِرْ عَلَيْهِ بِمَا تَعْلَمُ
أَنَّهُ يُقَرِّبُكَ إِلَى اللَّهِ تَعَالَى.»

Abū Ḥanīfah رحمه الله said:

"Don't be stingy as [stinginess] makes a person hated."

Personal Reflections

قال أبو حنيفة رحمه الله:

«وَإِيَّاكَ وَالبُخْلَ، فَإِنَّهُ يُبْغَضُ بِهِ المَرْءُ.»

ABŪ ḤANĪFAH رَحِمَهُ ٱللَّٰهُ SAID:

“Don’t be greedy, a liar, or one who mixes up [matters or information], rather compose yourself in all situations.”

PERSONAL REFLECTIONS

قال أبو حنيفة رَحِمَهُ ٱللَّٰهُ:

«وَلَا تَكُ طَمَّاعًا وَلَا كَذَّابًا، وَلَا صَاحِبَ تَخْلِيطٍ، بَلِ احْفَظْ مُرُوءَتَكَ فِي الأُمُورِ كُلِّهَا.»

Abū Ḥanīfah رحمه الله said:

"Don't give your belongings to just any tailor or any craftsman, rather pick someone trustworthy to do it for you."

Personal Reflections

____

____

____

____

____

____

قال أبو حنيفة رحمه الله:

«وَلَا تُسَلِّمِ الأَمْتِعَةَ إِلَى الحَائِكِ وَسَائِرِ الصُّنَّاعِ، بَلِ اتَّخِذْ لِنَفْسِكَ ثِقَةً يَفْعَلُ ذَلِكَ.»

ABŪ ḤANĪFAH رَحِمَهُ ٱللَّهُ SAID:

“If you happen to be amidst a people, don’t advance before them to lead prayer if they themselves don’t respectfully push you forward.”

PERSONAL REFLECTIONS

____

____

____

____

____

____

قال أبو حنيفة رَحِمَهُ ٱللَّهُ:

«وَإِذَا كُنْتَ فِي قَوْمٍ، لَا تَتَقَدَّمْ عَلَيهِمْ فِي الصَّلَاةِ مَا لَمْ يُقَدِّمُوكَ عَلَى وَجْهِ التَّعْظِيمِ.»

Abū Ḥanīfah رَحِمَهُ الله said:

"Don't keep two wives in one house."

Personal Reflections

قال أبو حنيفة رَحِمَهُ الله:

«وَلَا تَجْمَعْ بَيْنَ امْرَأَتَيْنِ فِي دَارٍ وَاحِدَةٍ.»

ABŪ ḤANĪFAH رحمه الله SAID:

"Don't get married until you are sure that you are capable of fulfilling all of her needs."

PERSONAL REFLECTIONS

____

____

____

____

____

____

قال أبو حنيفة رحمه الله:

«وَلَا تَتَزَوَّجْ إِلَّا بَعْدَ أَنْ تَعْلَمَ أَنَّكَ تَقْدِرُ عَلَى القِيَامِ بِجَمِيعِ حَوَائِجِهَا.»

Abū Ḥanīfah رحمه الله said:

"Seek knowledge first, then collect permissible wealth, and lastly get married."

Personal Reflections

قال أبو حنيفة رحمه الله:

«وَاطْلُبِ العِلْمَ أَوَّلًا، ثُمَّ اجْمَعِ المَالَ مِنَ الحَلَالِ، ثُمَّ تَزَوَّجْ.»

ABŪ ḤANĪFAH رَحِمَهُ ٱللَّٰهُ SAID:

"Occupy yourself with knowledge in your youth whilst your heart and your mind are free [of other occupations]."

PERSONAL REFLECTIONS

قال أبو حنيفة رَحِمَهُ ٱللَّٰهُ:

«وَاشْتَغِلْ بِالعِلْمِ فِي عُنْفُوَانِ شَبَابِكَ، وَقْتَ فَرَاغِ قَلْبِكَ وَخَاطِرِكَ.»

Abū Ḥanīfah رحمه الله said:

“Even if you remain without earnings or provisions for ten years, don’t turn away from knowledge.”

Personal Reflections

قال أبو حنيفة رحمه الله:

«وَإِنْ بَقِيتَ عَشْرَ سِنَينَ بِلَا كَسْبٍ وَلَا قُوتٍ، فَلَا تُعْرِضْ عَنِ العِلْمِ.»

Abū Ḥanīfah رحمه الله said:

"If you turn away from knowledge, your livelihood will become constrained."

Personal Reflections

قال أبو حنيفة رحمه الله:

«فَإِنَّكَ إِذَا أَعْرَضْتَ عَنْهُ، كَانَتْ مَعِيشَتُكَ ضَنْكًا.»

Abū Ḥanīfah رَحِمَهُ اللهُ said:

"Seek forgiveness for [your] teacher and whoever you took knowledge from."

Personal Reflections

قال أبو حنيفة رَحِمَهُ اللهُ:

«وَاسْتَغْفِرْ لِلأُسْتَاذِ، وَمَنْ أَخَذْتَ عَنْهُ العِلْمَ.»

ABŪ ḤANĪFAH رحمه الله SAID:

"Adopt specific *awrad*[21] for yourself after prayer in which you recite the Quran, remember Allah, and thank Him for the patience He has instilled within you and the blessings that He has granted you."

PERSONAL REFLECTIONS

____

____

____

____

____

____

قال أبو حنيفة رحمه الله:

«وَاتَّخِذْ لِنَفْسِكَ أَوْرَادًا خَلْفَ الصَّلَاةِ تَقْرَأُ فِيهَا القُرْآنَ، وَتَذْكُرُ اللَّهَ -تَعَالَى- وَتَشْكُرُهُ عَلَى مَا أَوْدَعَكَ مِنَ الصَّبْرِ، وَأَوْلَاكَ مِنَ النِّعَمِ.»

21 A regiment of recitation, prayers, supplications, or other worship which is usually done at specific times, or on specific days. The singular of the word *awrād* is *wird*.

Abū Ḥanīfah رحمه الله said:

"Observe yourself."

Personal Reflections

قال أبو حنيفة رحمه الله:

«وَرَاقِبْ نَفْسَكَ.»

ABŪ ḤANĪFAH رحمه الله SAID:

“Persist on good so that you may benefit from your knowledge in this life and the next.”

PERSONAL REFLECTIONS

____

____

____

____

____

____

قال أبو حنيفة رحمه الله:

«وَحَافِظْ عَلَى الخيرِ لِتَنْتَفِعَ مِنْ دُنْيَاكَ وَآخِرَتِكَ بِعِلْمِكَ.»

Abū Ḥanīfah رحمه الله said:

“Don’t incline toward your worldly life, and the situation that you may be in as Allah will ask you about all of that.”

Personal Reflections

قال أبو حنيفة رحمه الله:

«وَلَا تَطْمَئِنَّ إِلَى دُنْيَاكَ، وَإِلَى مَا أَنْتَ فِيهِ،
فَإِنَّ اللهَ تَعَالَى سَائِلُكَ عَنْ جَمِيعِ ذَلِكَ!»

ABŪ ḤANĪFAH رحمه الله SAID:

"Remember death."

PERSONAL REFLECTIONS

قال أبو حنيفة رحمه الله:

«وَاذْكُرِ المَوْتَ.»

Abū Ḥanīfah رحمه الله said:

"Regularly recite [the Quran]."

Personal Reflections

قال أبو حنيفة رحمه الله:

«وَدَاوِمْ عَلَى التِّلَاوَةِ.»

ABŪ ḤANĪFAH رَحِمَهُ ٱللَّهُ SAID:

"Regularly visit graves, *shuyūkh*, and blessed places."

PERSONAL REFLECTIONS

____

____

____

____

____

____

قال أبو حنيفة رَحِمَهُ ٱللَّهُ:

«وَأَكْثِرْ مِنْ زِيَارَةِ القُبُورِ، وَالمَشَايِخِ، وَالمَوَاضِعِ المُبَارَكَةِ.»

Abū Ḥanīfah رحمه الله said:

"Wear white clothes in all situations."

Personal Reflections

قال أبو حنيفة رحمه الله:

«وَالْبَسْ مِنَ الثِّيَابِ البِيضَ فِي الأَحْوَالِ كُلِّهَا.»

ABŪ ḤANĪFAH رَحِمَهُ ٱللَّهُ SAID:

“Show the satisfaction of your heart.”

PERSONAL REFLECTIONS

قال أبو حنيفة رَحِمَهُ ٱللَّهُ:

«وَأَظْهِرْ غِنَى القَلْبِ.»

Abū Ḥanīfah رحمه الله said:

"Display affluence in [the way you carry] yourself."

Personal Reflections

قال أبو حنيفة رحمه الله:

«وَأَظْهِرْ مِنْ نَفْسِكَ الغِنَاءَ.»

ABŪ ḤANĪFAH رحمه الله SAID:

"Don't show your poverty even if you happen to be poor."

PERSONAL REFLECTIONS

قال أبو حنيفة رحمه الله :

«وَلَا تُظْهِرِ الفَقْرَ، وَإِنْ كُنْتَ فَقِيراً.»

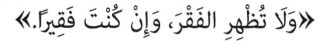

Abū Ḥanīfah رَحِمَهُ ٱللَّٰهُ said:

“Be resolute for he who has a weak resolve will have a low station.”

Personal Reflections

____

____

____

____

____

____

قال أبو حنيفة رَحِمَهُ ٱللَّٰهُ:

«وَكُنْ ذَا هِمَّةٍ، فَإِنَّ مَنْ ضَعُفَتْ هِمَّتُهُ ضَعُفَتْ مَنْزِلَتُهُ.»

ABŪ ḤANĪFAH رَحِمَهُ ٱللَّٰهُ SAID:

"Degrade the worldly life [in your eyes] just as it is insignificant to the people of knowledge because what Allah has in store is surely better than it."

PERSONAL REFLECTIONS

____

____

____

____

____

____

قال أبو حنيفة رَحِمَهُ ٱللَّٰهُ:

«وَحَقِّرِ الدُّنْيَا المُحَقَّرَةَ عِنْدَ أَهْلِ العِلْمِ، فَإِنَّ مَا عِنْدَ اللَّهِ خَيرٌ مِنْهَا.»

Abū Ḥanīfah رحمه الله said:

"Don't become angry in the gatherings of knowledge."

Personal Reflections

قال أبو حنيفة رحمه الله:

«وَإِيَّاكَ وَالغَضَبَ فِي مَجْلِسِ العِلْمِ.»

Abū Ḥanīfah رحمه الله said:

"Don't become a storyteller for the masses as a storyteller has to lie."

Personal Reflections

قال أبو حنيفة رحمه الله:

«وَلَا تَقُصَّ عَلَى العَامَّةِ فَإِنَّ القَاصَّ لَا بُدَّ لَهُ أَنْ يَكْذِبَ.»

BIBLIOGRAPHY

BIBLIOGRAPHY

❖ al-Baghdādī, al-Khāṭīb, Edited by Bashār ʻAwwād Maʻrūf, Beirut: Tarīkh Baghdād. Dār al-Gharb al-Islāmī, 2002.

❖ al-Barsījī, Muḥammad al-Sayyid, Min Waṣāyā al-Imām al-Aʻẓam, Amman: Dār al-Fatḥ, 2013.

❖ al-Bukhārī, Muḥammad Ibn Ismāʻīl, Ṣaḥīḥ al-Bukhārī, Edited by Khalīl Maʼmūn Shīḥā, Beirut: Dār al-Maʻrifah, 2004/1425.

❖ al-Dhahabī, Shams al-Dīn, *Siyar Aʻlām al-Nublāʼ*. Edited by Shuʻaib al-Arnaʼūṭ, Beirut: Muʼassasat al-Risālah, 1985.

❖ al-Qārī, Al-Mullā ʻAlī, *Sharḥ Musnad Abī Ḥanīfah*. Beirut: Dār Al-Kutub Al-'Ilmīyah, 1985.

❖ al-Qushayrī, Muslim ibn al-Ḥajjāj, Edited by Naḍhar al-Fāriyābī, *Ṣaḥīḥ Muslim*. Riyadh: Dār Ṭaybah, 2006.

❖ al-Ṣaymarī, al-Husain Ibn ʻAlī, *Akhbār Abi Ḥanīfah Wa Aṣ-ḥābihi*. Beirut: ʻĀlam al-Kutub, 1985.

❖ Shams, Muḥammad Rashād Manṣūr, *al-Madkhal ʼIlā al-Madhhab al-Ḥanafī*, Damascus: Dār al-Nahḍah, 2006/1427.

❖ al-Shaʻrāni, ʻAbdul Wahhāb, *al-Mīzān al-Kubrā al-Shaʻrāniyyah*. Beirut: Dār al-Kutub al-ʻIlmiyyah, 1998.

❖ al-Tirmidhī, Muḥammad Ibn 'Īsā, Edited by Bashār ʻAwwād Maʻrūf, *al-Jāmiʻ al-Kabīr*, Beirut: Dār al-Gharb al-Islāmī, 1996.

❖ al-'Uthmānī, Ẓafar Aḥmad, *Iʻlāʼ al-Sunan*. Beirut: Dār Iḥyāʼ al-Turāth al-ʻArabī, 2013.

❖ Shams, Muḥammad Rashād Manṣūr, *al-Madkhal ʼIlā al-Madhhab al-Ḥanafī*, Damascus: Dār al-Nahḍah, 2006/1427.

NOTES

Notes

....

....

....

....

....

....

....

....

....

....

....

....

Printed in Great Britain
by Amazon

40191276R00071